LOCAL

**A POETRY COLLECTION
(2001 to 2016)**

By

Peter Dean

All poems copyright Peter Bernard Dean 2016 ©

WOBBLE (2001)

Jelly

Wobble.
Green, red, yellow,
Wobble.
Breast firmness.
Touch it,
Wobble it,
Eat it –
Jelly.

Hair

Combing my
Dark, greasy hair,
It waves and curls.
"You look like a Beatnik!"
Calls my brother.
I washed it last week,
But hair is a funny thing –
The shampoo never
Stays on long, and
Natural oils take over
Within a couple of days.
"I'm not worth it!" I think,
And dream of peace
And tranquillity.

Songbird

The songbird flies,
Harmless –
"Freedom for all!" it cries
As it soars.
The man builds a cage
Out of fine bamboo,
And all is lost.

WinterBeach Scene

Driftwood lying at the beach head,
Yellow sand, mottled pebbles –
Amber amongst them.
A high tide lashing
An empty beach.
Foam.
Some spray as from a can
Scenting the air.
Gulls flying near the cliff face,
Calling incessantly in the cold –
Painful shrieks,
Like a drowning man.

Monday

We had it all –
 Good food and wine
And glorious days.
But after the party
Breaks up,
And time disappears,
I don't think I'll make it
To Monday.

Murder Mystery Whodunnit?

Your head
Bathed in blood:
Pooling,
Warm, still warm.
In life
You were magnificent –
Riding with the Gods:
Apollo's hair,
Leaping horses.
In death,
A silent heap
Lying at the foot
Of the marble stairs,
Your head
Cracked open,
Beside a broken vase.

Lady Frank –
Francis Appleton –
Had no motive
Bar an undisclosed debt of £500,000,
Owed by the victim's father,
Once a dollar billionairess,
Now merely a millionairess,
She lived like a leopard,
But was too caring
To kill such a
Young, young man.

Baron Harding
On the other hand
Was a beast with money,
And had no sexual
Morals to speak of –
Whoring
In Amsterdam,
Where diamonds
Come cheaper than

Some of the wild nights.
He needed no motive,
But had one all the same –
The victim was his
Secret, secret illegitimate son.

Penny Phillips,
A young teenage maid,
As pretty as the lakes
On which the house overlooked.
She knew the victim's
Thighs and chest,
And recently carried his seed.
Her motive was
Spurned love, for sure,
Or was her father's
Fury enough
To extinguish her fire?

We look at you,
Your head bathed in blood –
Pooling: warm, still warm.

A sleuth arrives
To take notes
Whilst photographs flash.
A statement is taken
From each suspect,
Just as the gong sounds,
And dinner is served
In this stately home –
With one place missing.

Great Big Tree

Great big tree,
One hundred years old,
Or more …
What have you seen?
What secrets do you tell?
Who loves who
On your bark?
Oak:
Quercusrobur is proper.
Dominate me in the forest.
Let in the mottled light,
Provide sanctuary
For many creatures under your canopy.
You're as English as Elgar
But quite a foreigner to our cities now,
Banished to country parks
And fields where big tractors
Plough and sow seed
For the people.
Your reign is a long one, undestroyed.
It is a history of weather –
Unopened.
Until your demise
In some freak storm
Or by the saw of uncaring beasts.
The lovers, divorced by now,
The secrets suddenly revealed,
And the country one big tree less –
And how much wiser.

Above A Summer Meadow

Above a summer meadow
A skylark serenades
And watches as the sugar-sap of a peach-fruit
Dribbles down your chin.
My senses numbed from pure delight
Of rivers ambling down a hillside
Whilst horses run free,
And rabbits dance around their burrows.
A picnic by the meandering stream
Frames our picture of calm,
And eternity melts to a second
As you smile once more.
Intense is the perfume of wine
When mixed with honey-dew:
And laughter reigns, above all else,
In the richness of this august heaven.

People Of A Certain Age

People of a certain age
Lay down their sticks,
Pull on cloaks of silk,
And sing from the mountaintops:
"I'm alive!"
Echoes through the valley
Cause trees to shudder.
Bears rise up on haunches
To rip at the bark.
Multiply yourself!
But be prepared my child
Your feet are soft and bare.
When you walk on the forest floor
Twigs will crackle and snap,
Alerting the kestrel's eye.

Philosophical About Builders

Them geezers said the job's too hard
To get all done in just one day:
"Ain't got the tools 'ere in our bag,
Sorry mate," I heard them say.
But still they stayed,
And still they played
That blasted radio all day.
And whistled to the mindless tunes
And used a rule
Instead of spoons,
To stir their tea
At ten and three.
And then they went home at four
Leaving shavings on the floor,
And did not even stop to say –
Oh well, they'll be back another day.

Beauty

The beauty seen in your mother's face
Gives a pure white swan the power
To glide on a mirrored lake.
The lake stretches for miles
Before the rocky rapids,
And waterfall
Disperse the shine.
But your beauty remains
In every waking second I count,
And every sleeping hour
When I dream,
And see your mother's face.

A Kerouac Dream

If only I could have met 'ol Jack!
I'd like to slap him on the back,
Buy him a beer, and say:
"How you doin' there?"
And we'd just walk, and talk about books
And the whole futility of things -
Buddies firing down the highway
Into the heartbeat of America,
Circa 1956.

And so with dharma dreams in mountain glades
Lawrence, Allen, Gregory and co
Joined the high-priest, who
Once soared with angels across a warring sea,
And they smote the world a deathly blow,
By testaments, before the rise of Dylan,
To guide a nation of waifs
Onto the dusty road.

Until space frontiers burst their banks
And swinging Sixties roared, again,
To excessive tones of lust, and drink, and drugs –
And music from the stars.
"Heard it all before," murmured the man
From his infirmary bed,
Haemorrhaged and sinking fast
On October twenty one.
Elusive Jack Duluoz, old breed pioneer,
Finally, in life, was no more.

One Spring

Spring is wonderful!
Forgotten sunshine
Radiates on emerging flowers.
Vivid shields of colour on the palette
Aside the green willow, overhanging
The river's edge.
New buds bursting like balloons –
And a white rabbit from a hat!
Cool winds don't dampen the excitement
Of does and bucks in the shadow of Eden.

I remember you
In your pink tassely dress.
You were alive to me,
With keen embraces and hot fire kisses.
In the short time of passion, back arched,
Your hands tugging clumps of Chelsea blue *Muscari.*

Long ago,

One Spring.

Looking After Wildlife

A cat has claws to catch birds and mice
They really have little chance,
Once in the night-sights
Of the one who'll be King,
When he's made his brutal advance.

Curl up by the fire, or on mother's lap
Purring for all that he's worth.
Forgetful are we
To the killer within,
But his victims are lined up on the earth.

Most people love their cat as their own
And get upset and uptight,
When young Tiddles
(or old George, by the by),
Are locked up indoors at dusk, overnight.

But it's the only way to cut down on death,
Let the garden wildlife survive.
The cat is not there,
But asleep in a chair,
Whilst the dawn chorus of birds is alive.

Mindset

Sailing close to the wind
Really does clear the mind.

Trust

Trust: Given without advice –
        Taken without asking.

Rebel Youth

I watch the joss-stick burn down
While listening to whale sounds,
And I think the world is beautiful.
My long hair needs combing.
Shall I chant – or leave it today?
I think I'll leave it,
But rearrange the cushions
On which I sit, cross-legged.

Thunderstorm

Electric light, rocket-like burst,
Kills a day.
White electric shock wave.
Crash,
Light, light.
Boom!
Steamroller o'er the sky.
Grey cloud, flattening ogre,
Wilderness light.
Crash,
Light, light,
Crash.
Boom!
Dragon's tears flood to ground,
Pitiful, cold,
Under a shaded sun, sadness sun, mournful sun.
Crash,
Light, light,
Crash.
Boom!
Electric light,
Rocket-like burst.
Blue-cloud flattening,
Wilderness light,
Pitiful, cold,
Under a shaded sun, sadness sun, mournful sun.
Crash, crash,
Light, light...
BOOM!!!

Fingers

Guitar playing is a skill he developed
Aged 13 ½ -
In band practice lessons.
He went on to master
The sax and the drums,
And play a big role in smoky jam sessions.

He later read music,
The notes on a page,
And studied at Art school
With money he'd saved.
One song he felt should drop down a key
To fit his voice,
Now aged twenty three.

Always confident on the outside,
But a sensitive soul
When in a crowd.
Creativity brought him local fame,
In venues where people knew of his name.
His fingers flowed in rhythm and beat,
On any instrument,
In pubs, clubs, even out on the street.

But heroin got him
When thirty years old,
He o/d'd one winter's night
And died in the cold.

Buried now, so that all can see
Young 'Finger's' grave, surrounded by trees.
But his local legend lives on, he will never grow old,
Because when Fingers stopped playing
They broke the great mould.

Young Love

Brown eyes flashing like a lamp,
Coral lips do smile.
Arm in arm, hand in hand,
Along the seaside mile.

Stopping for cockles and some shrimp,
Taste of salty sea.
Feeding you with a plastic fork,
Whilst you were feeding me.

Strolling on the beach by the waves,
Discarded shoes and socks.
Kissing your lips gently now,
Warm wind running through long locks.

This was when our love was young,
Freedom did prevail.
A hug reassured, no symbolic ring
To catch us by the tail.

The Bumble Bee

"The bumble bee technically can't fly,"
So Roger Mc Gough said,
"But it does!" he goes on
In a poem I've read.

Does the lark wake up
Early each morn?
And catch the first worm
Before feasting on corn?

And the robin who has
Such a red breast,
Disappears in the summer
To have a good rest.

Natural possibilities
In the blink of an eye,
Evolution is working
Under the royal blue sky.

I Am Inside

I am inside,
Feet curled, eyes closed.
I cannot think, I drink your blood,
I'm in the dark.
I want to taste the sun
As it shines on the outside,
Bursting.
I am inside.

Drunk On The 10th Floor

All the best feelings in the world
Gather to congregate in him –
The drunk on the 10th floor.
Playing air trombone,
And double bass,
To a tune on the radio.
Beating Sinatra to a high note.
The neighbours thump the floor.
He clicks the radio off,
"Shhhh!"
He clicks the radio on,
Takes another slug of spirit.
Changes from air sax to trumpet
And drums – arms flying everywhere,
Pah-pahping away,
The drunk is content, living in his rooms, high up,
On the 10th floor.

Mother's Day

What thought's are conjured by Mother's Day?
Thoughts of warmth, and kindness, and flowers,
Spring flocks of lambs in fields today
Skipping away the hours.
Mother's are kissed by children fair,
Adorned with love and devotion,
Praising the women, who in their care
Gave them life, and hope, and motion.
So love your mother where 'ere she be,
For your life be her best friend,
She'll give you her love, returned for free,
On that you can always depend.

Late Winter

Ice melts as wind warms,
But the night still freezes.
Snow is here by dawn,
Glowing as daylight teases.

Jack Frost cracking the hard, dark ground,
Let shoots of life push through,
Then grow, as watered sun is found
And snowdrops shine in dew.

A blanket of crocus and daffodil
As the temperature rises,
Seasons move on, they always will,
And give us more surprises.

A Prayer For Love

Adorable you,
How fine your parted lips –
Kiss me slowly.
Let me drown in emotion,
Whilst you melt.
Let me hang in peril,
Your every move.
I want to be with you
From this moment
Till the end of time.
A simple prayer
For your love
Always.

The Teenage Punk Rocker

Back in the Punk Rock days of my youth
Penetration and Sex Pistols looked for the truth.
Spitting and bondage trousers were the fashion,
Mohican hair was dyed like red Russian.
London Calling and White Riot on the streets,
Don't dictate to me when we meet.
Underground bands in underground bars
Couldn't play their music with their guitars.
But I got hooked on all of this,
It was at a punk concert I had my first kiss.
A small girl with a studded collar and black eye make-up
Snogged me whilst I grasped at her velvet purple jacket.
I got no further than touching her bra,
A public fumble to drown out those guitars.
No sexual intercourse after fore play,
She rejected me in a mean, callous way.
I saw her walking down our busy street
With two crying children down at her feet.
It made me wonder of what might have been
If we had made love when just a teen.
The things we do when we are so young
Come back to haunt us, but we did have fun.
Yes, fun in the 70s when we were sixteen
True love, just learning, together it seems.

Man Eaters

Lovely women in our town,
Walking, talking, laying rules down,
On how to shop, or make up with boys,
Playing with life and all of life's toys.
These lovely women really do know
What it's like to mature in status, and grow,
They have men for breakfast, lunch and tea –
And I should know, they humiliated me.
Living by some weird 'feminist' rules,
Drinking, swearing, playing the fool,
In pubs and night clubs for all to see,
On Friday nights, out on the scene.
Ladettes by any other name -
Hooligans put the sweet ones to shame.
Walking, talking, laying rules down,
Such lovely women there are in our town!

Crystal Eyes

Deep sea eyes,
Crystal blue,
Look at me,
I look at you.

Straw blonde hair
Tied back at times,
Flicking across
Your face so fine.

Your friendship is such
A good, cherished thing,
With all the joys
A good friend really brings.

So Miss crystal eyes
Shining blue,
Just look at me
And I at you.

Teapot

Teapot, teapot,
Hot, hot tea,
In the bag or leaf.
Teapot, teapot,
Let me get
A little light relief.

Teapot, teapot,
Tip me up,
Pour my liquid out.
Teapot, teapot,
Hold my handle,
But do not hold my spout.

Teapot, teapot,
Now to chores,
And business around the house.
Teapot, teapot,
Thanks so much,
I'll put you on the shelf.

Saturday

Why can't it be Wednesday?
I'm going dating on Wednesday night:
Second date!
She is like a custard slice.
I love custard slices!
I want to eat my slice,
And luxuriate in its taste.
Maybe we'll hug like last time
On saying 'Goodbye'?
Does she like me?
She won't say.
All I know is that here on Saturday
My stomach feels like custard,
And I know that on Wednesday night

My legs will freeze up, and resemble jelly.

Floodwater

Floodwater is coming,
For years it's the worst.
Floodwater is coming,
This land is just cursed.
Floodwater is coming
To houses and farms.
Floodwater is coming,
Everything harmed.
Floodwater is coming,
The old and the new.
Floodwater is coming,
Rain, not for the few.
Floodwater is coming,
People not giving thanks.
Floodwater is coming,
Rising levels, river banks.
Floodwater is coming
Drowning barley and wheat.
Floodwater is coming
Government is downbeat.
Floodwater is coming,
People do cry.
Floodwater is coming,
Hefting sandbags, they try.
Floodwater is coming,
The worst over, I fear,
Floodwater is coming,
Floodwater is here.

St Valentine's Day

What to do on St Valentine's Day?
Some chocs, or a meal in a big way?
A kiss and a cuddle would be such bliss,
Some loving words about that and this.

Champagne and roses, truffles, and bits,
The wood stove so hot, the room candlelit.
Romantic chatter in a nice home
Would be a dream for me alone.

But because I am single, have been for so long,
I'll listen to music, get lost in a song,
Have a beer, a chip butty, have nothing to say,
Watch TV in the corner, this St Valentine's Day.

Spuds

Buttery mash,
Chips or hash,
With peas and fish,
Or pies in a dish.
With eggs or mutton,
Sausages and onions.
There's no better grub put upon a plate,
Than piles of spuds, they are just great!

Essex Girls

She waddled
Like a duck -
In those high heels.

POETRY SUPERSTORE (2014)

Homecoming

Tell me when you can come on home
And I will warm the house,
Put wood in the grate, build up the fire
And banish ev'ry mouse.

It will be the greatest, joyous day
To see you and our son
Here in Fenland, back again
You know you are the one.

So celebrate with ale and wine
And cheese and grapes and bread
Our love has stood the test of time,
My heart still rules my head.

Come down from Leeds
Your mother's fine, she'll live another day
I missed you dearest, and our son,
Two weeks have gone astray.

I long to hear your voice again
I missed the boy's young smile
Wanting, yearning, all through the day
I count your every mile.

The cat has gotten
Used to me, and my slack, slack ways,
He sleeps and eats and scratches chairs,
In his mournful daze.

Now it's three and you arrive
I hear the car pull up,
The boy runs quickly, you get out,
In haste I fill my cup.

We kiss and hug
And laugh and sing as if we are new-born,
My legs go weak, my eyes feel tears,
We're happy through 'till dawn.

Now we are three
A family here, overcoming time apart,
Love boldens me, our fire ignites,
Two joyous, beating hearts.

January Morning

Winter.
The lady's cold, rheumatic fingers
Scratch away some ice
From her windows.
Some children in the street throwing snowballs.
Clunk! Snow hits the wall, and sticks,
Freezing into chunks of ice.
"Clear off!" the lady screams,
"Get away from here!"
She lifts her stick at the boys.
Snowballs lobbed in the air –
One hits the window.
Plop! The snow is soft this time,
Ice flakes drag down the pane.
"Clear off!" the lady screams,
But the children can't hear her,
Her voice is frail, like a breath –
Seen clearly on this icy-white January morning

Christmas night

Come, come, come and see,
What Santa Claus has brought for me.
A sack of wonder and of awe,
Christmas gifts, and so much more.

In candle-light, and on my knees,
I did propose, she was a tease.
She thanked me, but said: "I don't know,"
Before she smiled, and reached down low.
She took my hand and squeezed it, thus,
We hugged and kissed, without much fuss.
She shouted "Yes, I want you too!"
"I love you, dearest," my heart renewed.

A ring for love on Christmas night,
Engagement to my dear delight.
A kiss from her makes my heart sing,
My love forever is everything.

Peace

TV on in the corner.
Empty glass vase on a forgotten shelf.
Hyacinths growing slowly on a window sill.
Sofa hiding hidden treasures down its crevices.
Warm pile of carpet on the floor.
Ash-tray freshly emptied.
Father smoking his roll-ups.
Gas fire breathing heat into the room.
Peace.

The Farmer

The farmer stands in the bare-earth field,
A solitary figure under the balmy, warm sunshine of spring.
The whipping winter winds have passed,
April's warming has changed things.
His basket laden with seed, ready for scattering
On the hungry soil, as
Gulls hover in the distance,
Plunging down, looking for nature's food.

Desolation in the Highlands,
The bleak field is brown and bare,
Fallow up till now.
The farmer is strong from a life-time of toil on this land.
Evenly he scatters the seed.
He will wait now for rain and sun, and a rebirth of green.
The land, fallow up till now, is transformed by the season's will.

A nonsense poem...

Thy'reMigwatch

Ubey folds thy Migwatch glows,
Destruthuley, uley bowls.
Askanth thereby estey my,
They'se doth destrey, destrey by.

Askanth thereby estey my,
Thy fullefthmastry doth destrey.
Comef purse, uley bowls,
Emeth thine livef someway rolls.

Ubey folds thy Migwatch glows,
I hafpersuethMigwatch foals.
My lorfdarftshalopestey morn,
Thaspersoofmountethdestreyforn.

Askanth thereby estey my,
I shalthmyselththarMigwatch try!

Twenty One Again

I love that coloured dress,
And those boots are really cool.
Twirl, my dear, twirl.
You look like a true bohemian.
I bought you a necklace and some ear-rings,
With peridots.
Smile, my dear, smile.
That's better.
Take my hand and let's walk along the riverside.
Fidel can come too, bounding after his ball.
Put on your duffel coat, there is a little mist.
Let's skip along the towpath
To refresh ourselves.
Looking forward to the party tonight,
Singing at midnight.
Twenty one again.

Full Moon

Under the bright, full moon,
Mice scurry and chatter.
A hedgehog moves sprightly across the lawn.
Worms pop up from their burrows,
Whilst cats prowl and hunt.
A gentle breeze ruffles the leaves on the silver birch.
Owls hoot in the background
And I arrive in my car,
 Look up, and stare in amazement
At the greatness of the stars
And the wonder of this bright, clear, full moon.

Newborn

Brilliant times in the home,
Just a playful baby
And me.
Brilliant times all alone,
Just a tearful baby –
You'll see.
Brilliant times in the home,
Just a stinky baby
And me.
Brilliant times all alone,
Just a gleeful baby -
You'll see.
Brilliant times in the home,
Just a teething baby
And me.
Brilliant times all alone,
Such a bundle of joy
To see.

When You Cry

When you cry, I bleed inside.
Shaken like a young boy
For stealing a chew,
Your tears leave me dry.

When you play, I leap inside.
Rolling like a thunder cloud
On a summers eve,
Your smell in the hay.

When you love, I well-up inside.
Surfing on your water
In a river of feeling,
Your heaven above.

When you torment, I jump inside.
Turning cartwheels, in knots,
Like a winged bat,
Your meaning is sent.

When you cry, I bleed inside.

Bills

Bills drop through my door
Like blue whales.
One, two, three;
Gas, electric, water.
And there's more;
Telephone and computer
On top of food, drink
And council tax.
Let me be,
I don't occupy much space.
A consumer – yes – but a small one.
I hurry to the bank
And empty my account with a card flick.
Another few months of grace
Before bills drop through my door again;
Blue whales drinking my account dry
Like a vast thirsty beast.

Playing with cats

Playing with Fluffy in the garden,
Her long, black coat is divine,
Shiny and soft, it mats and it clumps,
Combing – a job that is mine.

Playing with Tina in the garden,
Her ginger/white fur warm to touch,
Her playful paws, and dangerous claws,
Swipe a little too much.

Playing with Sox in the garden,
He rolls and tumbles for fun,
But don't treat him unkindly now children,
Or he will get up and run.

These cats have played in our garden,
Been part of our home for a while,
Fluffy, Tina and Sox, when we were still young,
Each gave us a whopping big smile.

Garden

How magnificent our garden is,
Full of life and full of green,
August colour, flowers and bees,
Watch now, careful, veg and bean.

Tobacco plants lilt and sway
The breeze is soft and warm,
A sunflower's yellow radiant disc
Shines above the lawn.

Cosmos reds and purple's are
Majestic 'neath the birch
Whose lime-green leaves hang down sublime
And give the birds a perch.

Fruit trees bear small plums and pears,
Apple and damson, goosegog and all,
Not sweet-enough to eat, as yet,
But will be picked as day-length falls.

So make the most of summers fare
Love the sight of green and gold,
The coloured flowers and harvest fruits,
In autumn, will be yours to hold.

Fleur

Fleur the flower nymph
Waits and waits
The winter months so hard, and
Flowers deep in mother earth
Start showing in the garden.

From her warm winter bed
Fleur comes round and opens up
The box lid and the soft padding,
She dances to the door, ajar,
And into moon-shine heading

For daffodils and crocus silk
Unfolding slowly, slowly,
Out she gets her paints and brush
And with a swish
She colours, hush!

Yes hush the wind, and hush the rain
So delicate art may carry
In the early hours of late dawn,
Yellow hues and purple's
Cry out for life, Fleur has forsworn.

Let's cheer up from here on
There really is just one way now
To summer and the autumn fruits
Fleur paints the colours
Of plants whose roots

Stay firmly hidden in the soil,
Watered, sunshine-filtered good,
Fleur the flower nymph, busy now,
Her summer paints will not fade.
Hiding honey bees, showing how

To pollinate and produce
Seeds and fruits so huge,

To keep the garden so serene,
Colours burst, Fleur is the queen.

As winter puts out fronds of ice
In wind and on the hardened soil
Frozen plants die, flowers freeze
Fleur returns inside the house
The box whose wool surrounds her knees.

Fleur the flower nymph
Waits and waits,
The winter months so hard, and
Flowers deep in mother earth
Start showing in the garden.

Being Single

The night air is getting heavy
Dogs are barking at the cars
Summer sun has dropped from view
Now the moon shines with all the stars.
I kiss you twice and make you smile
Our hands touch and intermingle
Fingers gently on fingertips
Clamp the feeling, being single.

A distant fly buzzes manically
A raindrop hits the open panes
A storm is brewing in the distance
Muggy air is what remains.
I bury my nose into your nape
And breathe amongst your brunette hair
Snuggling clean and so serene
You giggle and moan softly there.

We make love as the dogs still bark
Sweat and dark and rain that falls
Like wild beasts on a mountain peak
We share the joy and shout our calls.
Until the moon falls like a stone
And sun enters the open pane
I gasp and kiss your wanton mouth
I know that being single I can't remain.

Belle Exposed

Belle exposed.
Her curls of spiders' hair,
And pappus goose bumps.
Enchanted lips, coral colour.
Rosebud eye shadow counters a pale complexion.
Stepping into the frigid sheets
I lay beside my Belle,
Touch her décolletage with my nuzzling nose,
Tongue agape, wanting more.
She wraps her young digits around my lazy horn,
She strokes me gently,
I climb her thin thighs whilst she sighs helplessly,
Eyes shut, the rosebud eye shadow peeping like a
Butterfly warning,
Until it is finished.
She smiles broadly whilst
White horses crash and disperse,
Rampant and fresh
Like the sea grabbing the golden sands.

Bed

We played like children in our soft, old bed,
But now the spearing from a metal spring
Hits me in the back.
Jutting out into the small of my back,
Where you once massaged me
Before our love came undone.

Moving to avoid the spring
I feel you again,
Touching, yes pushing my back with cool fingers.
I curl up beside you, on my side,
But the spring pokes through,
Like a thick, silver needle.
I kiss your spine,
You permit me that, in the dark.
You realise I want more,
With my dreaded hand, claw-like, grabbing,
Over your shoulder,
"Stop!" you call, "Stop!"
I turn over again, forgetting the spring,
And get a sharp reminder
Of what pain can be.

Cats

Cats sleep anywhere,
Any table any chair,
Open drawer,
Window ledge,
In the garden,
Under hedge.
Purring as the sun shines bright,
A cat asleep a wondrous sight.
Flicking whiskers
Twitching toes,
Mousing just where 'ere he goes.
Cats sleep anywhere,
Fourteen hours without a care.
Garden birds and garden rats (stay clear),
Of king and queen,
Our garden cats

Don't Give Your Heart To Him, My Dear

Don't give your heart to him, my dear
You'll end up in a fix
For he is only twenty one
And you are forty six.

You may just want to mother him
Enthral him with your tricks
But don't give your heart to him
As you are forty six.

A dream that he will marry soon
And live happy does not stick,
As when he is only thirty one
You will be fifty six.

You want to give your all to him
A fling could be in the mix
Dance with a man of twenty one
Will make your heels just click.

But is it worth the heart-ache, my dear
Someday he'll make his picks
He'll choose a girl of twenty one
And not of forty six.

Emily And The Band

My shirt is a bright turquoise blue,
With trousers pressed and brown in hue,
I wear my new white sneakers too,
To look as cool, as cool as you.

I never, ever wear a tie,
As it wraps my neck tight and so high,
And when I run I really fly,
Touching rainbows in the bright, bright sky.

We skip along, hand in naked hand,
Feeling so very, very grand,
We're going to see a young folk band,
On Uncle Tom's green grass farm land.

Banjo's, bass, guitar and strings,
Let us dance and we hear them sing,
It is a jolly, jolly thing,
In summer, down by the spring.

And then I bravely steal a kiss,
Amongst the midnight, heavy mist,
In truth, you don't really resist,
These moments should ne'er be missed.

Remember how we both walked back
To our parents' homes, along the track?
The light rising, dust made you hack,
But we made it, never looking back.

My teenage years, in shirts of blue
And trousers brown, I think of you,
Little Emily and me, so cool, in hue,
Our first kiss, and a love that grew.

Green

We've all got to decrease our emissions
Of CO2 and the like,
Switch off our big televisions
Go down the street on a bike.
Be Green instead of being greedy,
Recycle all manner of things,
Our life must be sustaining
So our children are taught about bins.

Green ones and black ones,
Sometimes blue,
Each for something, like cardboard or food.
Go to the waste site and get gobbled up,
Come back to us then, newspaper to cup.

Ecology, wind farms, wave-power could be
The future preoccupations to save all the trees.
And nuclear power, its waste slowly decays
So must be dismissed without any delays.

Oh men in power, you must now be seen
To push forward technology, so we can go Green!

Invisible Ghost

Long years have gone,
Your picture disperses in the murk
Of a pond.
A wave of water,
Mud merging with green.
Voodoo, hoodoo,
Don't play with me, friend.
Cautious smiles on the swings
In the park,
Infectious laughing
From the cemetery nearby.
Everywhere you are near,
Invisible ghost.

Love, Coming And Going
Love makes you froth and bubble,
Like a beckoning foam bath.
When love ends, hurt spikes
Like a thick needle piercing a buttock.
Longing and emptiness go on and on –
Days, weeks, sometimes years.
Strangers are mistaken for friends,
Someone you once knew well.
They go, you are left to soak,
Alone in the cold foam
Until your head and heart are heal.

Lament

Like a poppy flowering on the battlefields,
You are remembered.
Taken from me as love was blossoming,
The poppy shines in my heart.
A love gone, one true love.
I survive and ache,
But knowing you are blooming
Makes me smile.
I love you, as you were,
Here, forever.
Yes, I love you now
My poppy flower.

Life Goes On

One day, redundancy calls.
I have nothing to do, so I try
A hobby I've always wanted to try.
Model making has an appeal of hours,
Not days, and I'm too old for football practice.
I remember when my time was a premium,
I had the full diary of an important person,
Never thinking 'the Company' would break up
And cull livelihoods,
Like mine.
Thirty years of grind!
Retraining is all the rage,
I'm 52: no dog, no tricks, but
Too early to give up.
I think I'll be an eagle-eyed magpie
Selecting sparkly things.
An antique dealer of sorts,
A lover of beauty.
Self-employment, so grandiose.
With luck, we can retire to Marbella,
My wife and I.
Live life like peacocks by the Mediterranean Sea.
Spreading our feathers, at parties,
Into multi-coloured fans,
And running around in our old age
Knowing we're not for the chop,
Yes, knowing we're much too lucky for
Something as life-changing as that,
Just yet!

My Music

Walking down the coastal path
Guitar slung over my aching shoulder;
I stop.
I hear a blackbird calling,
Amid the sound of sea lapping the rocks on the shore.
I get out my mouth harp and play a few notes.
The bird stops,
Flies off into the day
And I'm all alone.
Strum the guitar like a far-out Dylan;
Attract a crowd in town.
Pigeons too,
On the rooftops.
Music seems to lull their senses.
The people give me some dull applause.
Pigeons,
They mess, white, in my upturned fedora.
Not for everyone, my music,
I guess.

Crowds

Where are you, my long, lost girl?
Living in a haze, my mind suddenly opens.
I see you again.
We dance and hug and kiss.
We make love on a veranda in a tropical storm.
I bathe with you
In coconut milk.
But it is all a dream.
Sadly, my love is not here.
She is in a crowd, somewhere,
So I call her name: Samantha!
Her ears prick up and she calls back: Peter!
Battling to the bus stop, the number 7,
We meet and steal a peck.
My mind clears and we board the bus
Together, heading for home, six stops away.

Nigel & Me

Nigel likes to talk about planes
And trains and motorbikes.
He has a few friends
Who like the same.
I say to him, Nige, Why does the piston go up and down?
He tells me,
But I don't really understand.
I go back to my poetry books
And let my imagination soar,
While Nigel gets on his bike and makes it roar.

Bicycle Wheels

Bicycle wheels go round,
The pedalling does me good,
Makes me lose a few pounds
Or, at least, I'm told it should.

Music

Music enters my ears
And eats away
Problems –
Soothing, bathing, caressing,
Until tears flow
Or the ego grows...
Let's play air guitar!
Music takes us over,
Now that is crazy.

Politician

The child screams
At the top of his voice:
"Liar, Liar, pants on fire!"
What insight into the adult world
For a politician's son to make.

Upper Social Circles

Do I want to move in upper social circles?
Have cucumber sandwiches
On green manicured lawns
 Talking about politics and art?
Or do I belong with the common man?
Taking stock of everyday things,
Drinking tea from mugs,
Dunking soldiers into eggs,
Once their shells are busted?
Let's sing around the old Joanna
Like in World War 2,
Get some community spirit going.
So, do I want to move in upper social circles?
I like cucumber
But it's best eaten with the rind on,
I find the taste in my mouth is far more pleasing.

Gecko

I bought you a
Ceramic gecko
To put on your dresser.
I hope it'll remind you
Of our student days
When we used to play in bed,
With me squeezing your leg
And pretending to be a
Little lizard climbing up your
Torso. You'd laugh and
I'd kiss you
Like I had never kissed you before,
Or will do again.
Now we are adults
And all you have to
Remind you of those heady days is
A ceramic gecko –
A little gift.

No Rain

A black cat meows at the sky
And goes inside again.
Native North American Indians try harder,
Still no rain.
Warm beautiful sunshine
Dries the soil further,
Wicked winds blow away precious seedlings.
Lucky, the black cat meows again
In the hope of striking a thunderstorm.
We wait patiently
Until the clouds break.

An Ant

An ant is an unassuming thing,
A being of wonderment,
A piece of a complete jigsaw.
Until, one fine summer's day
It grows wings and ups and flies away.

Games

Wondering when his time was up
The old man sits in his chair,
Grips the controls and launches a
Ball into the court on the telly.
He does like the Wii games.
Such a thing to keep him moving
And his brain active on a grey day
In the Home.

Remember

Remember those who fell in war,
Remember to the many more,
Who lost their limbs, and go before
Their comrades on the bloody shore.

Remember well my uncle Jack,
Who raised his gun and did attack,
The enemy firing rifles back,
Remember well my uncle Jack.

Remember then my auntie Jill,
Working nights up in the mill,
Producing bombs that sure will kill,
Remember well my auntie Jill.

Remember those who fell in war,
With poppies red upon the floor,
Stay in silence one minute more,
Remember those who fell in war.

Let The Flags Fly (Armistice Day)

Let the flags fly:
Old soldiers passing by.
Red, red poppies
Proudly displayed.
Let the flags be lowered
As poppies fall to earth:
Old soldier's heads bowed,
A tear for those who fell.
What Glorious war?
What distant land?
Remember them all
As our brothers and sisters,
In blood and mud,
Defying time.

Cold

Frost in the morning,
Haze in the air,
Ice on car windows,
Christmas is near.
November fireworks
Follows pumpkins and fright.
We must not forget
Clocks, and the sooner twilight.
Don't punish the homeless,
Out in the cold,
Give them warm shelter,
Some soup and whole food.
Be kind to the birds
Which appear in the garden,
They need fattening up
To stop them from starving.
And old people who live
With no heat on, I fear,
Need comfort and money
Now Christmas is near.

Gently, Gently

Gently, gently, the woman sleeps soundly.
Don't wake her,
Cradle her softly.
Kiss her forehead,
Brush away strands of hair from her face.
Kiss her ear,
Listen to her breathe.
Love her intensely.
Just watch.

Perfect

I think you're just perfect, my jigsaw piece
That fits me nicely, like sun in Greece.
I love your obsession with pretty things
It makes me warm, gives me wide open wings.
I love your curves and the way you move,
Your hair, your eyes, you have nothing to prove.
I'll love you forever, through rain, drought and snow
But my stomach is churning because I let you go.

The Author

Queued a blessed hour.
Terry, the author, chatted calmly,
Telling me he hadn't signed any other
Copies of this book, his first published tome.
He laughed and thanked me for coming.
The yellow-edged paperback,
A sorry state, with
Creased paper edges and torn cover,
Always reminds me of this word-smith
And his cinematic stories flashing in my head.

Madame

The bric-a-brac shop waits on Rue Nationale
In a sleepy French town.
It opens at ten,
And closes at one,
Till three,
Then on till seven in the evening.
Madame opens the shutters
Before going to feed her little dog,
Hettie.
Hettie's toenails clip clop on the ceramic tiles.
Madame feeds her green beans and tuna from a tin.
Hettie barks.
Madame sits at her counter
And waits for mail.
A customer comes in: "Bonjour!"
"Bonjour, ca va?"
A deal is done on a 1920s doll,
Three hundred euros until Christmas.
A good gift for a collector.
Madame is pleased, but no more customers today
As it is quiet.
Evening comes.
Hettie barks.
She eats and drinks,
Madame is always kind. Hettie knows.
She clip clops to her basket again.
Madame thinks about her man in England,
She smiles, but no-one sees.
She shuts the shutters and puts out the lights,
Another evening alone with Hettie and the TV.
Her man is waiting. Her man is waiting.

Winter Sun

See the sun through the winter haze,
It looks like liquid paint on these winter days.
The sun has no warmth amongst the rain,
But brightens the season in its pain.
Stretching across the mountain slope,
Shadows rush like an antelope.
Black panther clouds follow too,
Biting the legs of the foolish few.
Wishing spring would show its face,
End the time of winter's place.
See the sun through the winter haze,
The liquid paint just stays and stays.

Dinner

Oven on, it's time to cook
The shoulder of pork is prime.
Three hours of heat,
Crisp up the meat,
Add a touch of thyme.
Twenty mins, the veggies on,
Broccoli, carrots, peas,
Boil away, then simmer fine,
Just soft to fork to please.
Potatoes peeled and tossed in oil,
Oven-cooked, the most
 Crispy, delicious accompaniment
To our Sunday roast.

Office

Working till the evenings done
Aching bones and muscles too,
Lay a while, have some fun,
Drink and talk the late night through.

Missing sun in office trap,
No windows, breathe in conditioned air,
Machine coffee fills the gap,
Dierdre comes so close and stares.

She has a crush but won't let on,
The other workers know it's true,
But he is taken, he has gone
To sparkling lengths for faithful Sue.

Liam and brave Nigel May
Pull up ties and shine their shoes,
Cycle miles for Red Nose Day,
Raising cash to kill the blues.

Boss-man Liam makes his rules,
Poor Nigel lost his wife to Tim,
They knuckle down, work like mules,
Leaving problems in their bins.

Working till the evenings done
Aching bones and muscles too,
This office workforce will be gone
As unemployment comes into view

A New Beginning

Basking in ever rich rays
Tree buds, like pear, explode,
A rush of virginal-white and rose attract the ever-hungry bee.
A cacophony of colour deafens me,
Chills my bones like an angry wind
As earths dormant bulbs now flower.

Joyous hoots and calls,
A motorway of birdsong.
I love the spring, the green fertile spring.
The blossoms and scurrying creatures,
Frothing foam and sticks in fast-flowing rivers,
Moving in the warming breeze.

In summer, songs dim and fade
Around parched lanes at restful haze.
Growth of downy fruit and tom
Relaxing in ever-present shade.

I love the spring, the green fertile spring.
Old gentlemen come out and sing,
It purifies the soul.

Baby

Icky,
Yucky,
Squelchy,
Touchy,
Feely,
Gooey,
Sticky,
Lovely,
Baby,
You.

Ally's Bath-Time

Ally has fun in the bath,
She plays with her ducks, has a laugh.
The foam comes up to her ears,
And when the soap slips, she cheers.

Her mum puts the radio on,
The music is thumping along.
Ally whistles and sings
At the top of her voice,
As mum scrubs her back to the song.

Ally has fun in the bath,
She splashes the bubbles – not half!
Her mum tells her: "No, she must stop!"
But Ally insists she will not.

Her mum says "Ally's real clean,"
She lifts her out, to be seen.
Ally's dried all over,
And powdered in style,
And dressed in her night-shirt of green.

Tom's Big Day

Tom is going to be nine:
On the ninth day of the ninth month, in time,
Today he wakes with a cheer,
His birthday is now, really here.

Tom runs down the stairs of his home,
Mum and Dad have built a big dome,
His presents piled up on the floor,
Tom could not hope for anything more.

Opening a box on the top,
A racing car made him just stop,
Another big box is still there,
But hiding under a chair.

This box is opened in haste,
Tom tears the paper for waste –
A train set sparkles inside,
The box is so big and so wide.

A tear comes to little Tom's eye,
Mum and Dad stand and wonder just why?
The train set is perfect - what he'd choose,
His dream of this steam train, in blue.

Tom hugs his Mum and his Dad,
He is full of joy, so glad,
The train with track is his dream,
Going back to the days of hot steam.

Tom is nine today:
On the ninth day of the ninth month, Hooray!
Playing all day with his set,
It's a day he will never forget.

Four Seasons

In summer it gets very hot,
In winter it feels really cold,
In autumn leaves fly a lot,
In spring it's out with the old.

In summer the beaches are full,
In winter snow falls to the ground,
In autumn umbrellas are pulled,
In spring new flowers abound.

The seasons are in fours,
Here in Britain it is the folk lore.
But the cold and the rain
Will come again,
Once the sun and wind leave us once more.

Simon's Happy Family

Simon is watching TV.
He's as happy as he can be.

His dad is eating some kippers,
And wearing his smelly slippers.

His mum is on the phone
For an hour to Auntie Joan.

His brother is sucking his thumb,
Chewing it until it is numb.

Simon laughs at a TV joke,
His dad gives him a big poke.

His mum walks into the room,
While his brother looks up at the moon.

Simon is going to bed,
He has a story that just has to be read.

His dad finishes his supper of kippers,
And sniffs at his old smelly slippers.

His mum natters about Auntie Joan –
She has locked herself out of her home.

His brother is having his bath,
His toes go crinkly, he laughs.

Simon falls fast asleep,
His eyes close whilst counting some sheep.

His dad is now watching the News,
He is listening to other folks' views.

His mum checks the boys are okay,
She kisses them, "Nighty Night!" she says.

Simon dreams of some heavenly play,
His family are happy today.

The Land Of Nod, And Real Dreams

In the land of Nod, and real dreams,
Giants with beanstalks, and Queens,
Run around in the sky,
Hoping to try,
And scatter their magical beans.

Witches and elves are there too,
Looking for mischief to do,
Casting a spell,
Sticky spiders as well,
Are crawling, it's just what they do.

In the land of Nod, and real dreams,
You know things are not what they seem,
As you are tucked up asleep,
Some brave lions must keep,
You safe from all that is mean.

Pete's Diet

There was a young man named Pete,
Who was told he ate too much meat,
It'll make you too fat,
You can be sure of that,
So he went vegetarian all week.

His doctor said "This is fine,
You follow this diet of mine."
Carrots, broccoli, and rice,
He thought very nice
And his waistline began to decline.

Pete took to running as well,
To the bus stop, now he can tell,

His pork from his beans,
He eats lots of greens,
For his health is as sound as a bell.

Mary

Mary loved reading,
And sewing, and flowers,
She'd be with her books
Or her needles for hours.
Yes, Mary loved nature,
She'd look at the bees,
Draw and paint pictures
Of insects and trees.
She'd pick lovely blooms
And make perfume as well –
Rose petals in water –
Rose water with smell.
Now Mary loved reading,
And sewing, and flowers,
She'd be with her stories
Or her needles for hours.
She'd pick lovely blooms
And make perfume as well –
Rose petals in water –
Rose water with smell.

Cycling To Paradise

Pedal, pedal, pedal –
The hill is steep.
The sun perishes the tarmac.
Reach the top and
Wheeee!
Feet off the pedals,
Legs outstretched,
Freewheeling down.
Wind in hair,
Tentative hands on brakes,
Then stop at the junction.
Pedal, pedal, pedal –
Destination in sight.
Time for a drink
From the water bottle.
Cars go by; steel boxes.
Freedom comes from being alone
On the bike, cycling
To paradise.

Ecstasy

I feel like a sack of potatoes.
Stuck to my chair.
Heavy, no life.
Inanimate.
Half asleep.
Then you come and touch me gently.
My eyes open. Sparkling stars meet.
I leap up like a super-coiled spring.
Then, hot-stepping,
As light as flour sifted through a sieve,
Going round and round,
Fingers touching fingers -
A moment to treasure –
Ecstasy.

Lovely Garden

The garden plants in the plot
Are coming up, there's such a lot:
Peas and beans and spuds and leeks,
And in the warm, a superb peach.

The pretty flowers are in bloom
Making for an outdoor room.
Scented colours fill the air,
So you relax, without a care.

The hanging branches of the tree
Harbour insects on their leaves.
Birds come and peck to feed,
To keep the balance of nature free.

The lawn is cut every week,
And looks so good, a happy treat.
Stripes, the lines go up and down,
Like a putting green divine.

The pleasure of the great outdoors
Is to be had, both mine and yours.
Take in the view, breathe in a lot,
You will enjoy your garden plot.

Brighton Beach

Leester, Huge and me
On the Brighton trail.
Hop on a train to Portslade.
Try an all night breakfast.
Laugh and joke,
Pun and smoke,
Until the sun sets,
And the sea rests on the shingle.
Leester, Huge and me,
Discovering life –
Night swimming-
Feeling alive.

Meeting Up

Meeting up
At Martin's Coffee House,
Near the museum.
Shiny happy people
Go past,
Pushing elephants up the stairs.
You joke.
I laugh.
We smoke.
Heard the one about the vicar in the tutu?
And other sad humour.
You take your coffee strong and black,
I'm more mellow, with milk.
Don't talk about the weather –
Kafka is more interesting.
We plan to have a jam
With our guitars.
We are losing our religion
As slowly as we linger
Over our coffee.
Young people
Dreaming of Dylan,
And Beatniks,

In Martin's Coffee House,
Cambridge,
Near the museum.

Bluebell Wood

A bluebell mass is such a sight
In May, it sets the wood alight,
Covering the ground, the forest floor,
With vivid blue, can't ask for more.

Dappled sunshine cuts through the trees
The bluebells shimmer in the breeze,
The brilliant blue just hits the eye
Of any person passing by.

"Oh bluebell mass, you're such a sight
In May you set the wood alight."
I spoke these words with so much joy,
When I was just a little boy.

I saw the dappled sunshine rays
Through the trees, creating haze.
It stuck with me all these years,
And now it fills my eyes with tears.

A bluebell mass is such a sight,
In May, it sets the wood alight,
Covering the ground, the forest floor,
With vivid blue, who'd ask for more?

NATURE'S CAPERS (2014)

The Buzzing Bumble Bee

A bumble bee buzzes by
Swaying in the breeze,
Weighed down with nectar and honey dew
From flowers and from trees.

Pollinating trumpet flowers
Buzzing body bold,
Black, yellow 'fur', with white,
Bumble bees behold.

Foxgloves are a favourite plant
For this big buzzing chap,
Disappearing right inside the flower,
With just a little gap.

The bumble bee buzzes by
Flying through the air,
This solitary insect nests in holes,
Its food it doesn't share.

Buzzing bumble bees behold –
A truly lovely sight –
On spring and summer sunny days
In gardens and meadows bright.

An Earthworm Wriggles

An earthworm is a long, segmented creature,
For survival of life it is sure to feature,
Eating the earth and mixing things good,
Creating fertile topsoil in gardens and woods.

The earthworm has a number of hearts,
To break them is cruel, it really should hurt,
But does the earthworm have feelings as well?
Chomping on earth, it's hard to tell.

The earthworm is wriggly and really quite long,
For a wild creature it never does wrong,
We need it to fertilise our growing soil,
Like water and bread, our gas and our oil.

So treat an earthworm with respect it deserves,
It does us good – the soil it preserves,
Encourage it to do the work it does well –
Creating humus so the earth does not smell.

Fat Pigeons Cooing

Fat pigeons cooing on the lawn,
Flapping wings in some distress,
Eating grain put out at dawn
For blackbirds, robins, and the rest.

Clapping hands from open windows
Scare the fat blighters off,
The food is for the fledgling birdies,
Not the wastrels at the trough.

Pigeons take whatever's going,
Eating any grain or crust,
They call each other as if knowing,
Fluttering feathers, take or bust.

Clapping hands again disturbs them,
Stops them eating for a while:
"Go to someone else's garden,
Off you go, now make me smile!"

Pink And Purple Fuschia's: (an old lady's vision)

"Fuschia, Fuschia, flower for me!"
Said the old lady at noon.
"Fuschia, Fuschia, let colour be free!"
Pink and purple flowers will bloom.

"Fuschia, Fuschia, flower for me!"
The old lady said in high June.
"Fuschia, Fuschia please let me see
Flowers before the full moon."

"Fuschia, Fuschia, flower for me!"
And to the old lady's surprise,
Many Fuschia flowers can be seen,
Vivid colours before her poor eyes.

The Dangerous Wasp

The dangerous wasp creeps over a plum -
In autumn they are ruby and raw –
It feeds on the fruit, juicy and sweet,
Eating the flesh to the core.

Then flying outside to look for some more,
Sensing a child with ice cream,
It buzzes away, lands on the boy's hand,
And deposits its sting unseen.

The dangerous wasp makes the poor boy weep,
A puffy blotch burning his skin,
Mother bathes the hand, puts cream on as well,
And pulls out the wicked wasp's sting.

Lucky Money Spider

Money, money spider, the thread you weave,
Silken, strong and true.
Money, money spider, make me believe
My wishes through and through.

Money, money spider spun round my head,
Frenzied rope of silk.
Money, money spider, is it right
I've money under my quilt?

Money, money spider how did you know
My distant aunt has died?
Money, money spider, she was rich,
Her wealth is not denied.

Money, money spider, with your luck
My dreams have all come true,
The pot of money I have now
Gets me housing with a view.

Lilium

White lilies, red lilies, trumpeting here,
Shining all the day through.
Honey bees will soon appear,
With other insects too.

Lilium, Lilium, trumpeting here,
The summer is complete.
Lilies for the house, my dear,
The trumpets look so neat.

White lilies, red lilies, trumpeting here,
Triumphant to the last.
Tempting us when evening's clear,
A presence, oh so vast.

Lilium, Lilium, trumpeting here,
Beneath the summer sun.
Pleasing flowers far and near,
Till the day is done.

A Piggy-Wig At The Races

A piggy-wig is a-snuffling,
Searching through the mud.
Snorting, grunting, ruffling,
Covered in dirt and crud.

It's curly tail keeps waving
It's face and snout ahead.
Dig up the ground, then swaying
To its cider apple bed.

A piggy-wig is a-laying
On straw or grass or mud.
Snorting, grunting, swaying,
Near puddles from the flood.

But dress a pig in fine clothes,
Put polish on as well –
A hat, some shoes, well who knows?
The pig still emits a smell.

Grunting, snorting, laying,
At the races here.
A pig is a pig whose swaying
Is just what it appears.

Piggy-wig bets on number two,
At the very last race.
The jockey's shirt is Oxford blue,
He's ready for the chase.

Piggy-wig then grunts and he oinks,
The horse now romps home first.
Collects his cash, then doink! –
The pig is fit to burst.

A piggy-wig is a-snuffling,
Back on the farmer's land.
It's snorting and a ruffling,
Grunting – saying: "Grand!"

A Butterfly Smile

Bobbling about in the air,
A carefree ballet of play,
Red Admirals and Peacocks then share
Buddleia's flowers today.

Showing their wings to the sun
Whilst sipping plant fluids so sweet,
These butterflies basking for fun –
The Buddleia gives them their treat.

Some lemon yellows, and whites,
And those of a corn flower blue,
Float in a summer bright light,
Come to gardens and countryside too.

Fluttering off for a while
As cloud makes ever grey sky,
The butterflies' colours do smile,
And bring smiles to all passers-by.

Thirsty Little Aphids

Aphids suck the plants sap dry
They congregate on-masse,
Common black, or green, green fly
The tops of stems attacked.

Multiplying many fold,
Every minute, every hour,
Soapy water, so I'm told
Sprayed fast – like in a shower

Kills the pests in their tracks
Until those flying past
Drop on shoots and come on back,
They will not be the last.

But don't let aphids kill your plants –
Give them a soapy shower –
Beans and flowers will enhance
Your garden hour by hour.

Snuggling Broad Beans

The flowers are a nice black and white
With a lip for the bees,
The yellow pollen trips out so right
And pollinates with some ease.

Broad beans snuggle in their furry-lined pods,
Succulent veg to behold,
Broad beans cooked gently are a food for the Gods
When hot and even when cold.

Minty Potatoes

Potatoes are buried in the earth,
Fat tubers with shoots on called 'chits',
In April and May green leaves emerge
Growing fast until a frost hits.

In ten weeks' time they are ready,
On a plate in a quick whizz,
Fresh minty spuds get a culinary cheer,
Enjoyed by adults and kids.

After the new ones, the maincrop is here,
For mash, and roasties, and chips,
Potatoes are a staple food – it is clear –
We do love them all to bits!

Fragrant Rose

Roses have scent so divine,
Gardeners all seem to agree,
They majestically climb up like vines,
Or show off their wares as a tea.

Gertrude Jeykll is a favourite of mine,
It is of the old-fashioned breed,
The more you dead-head the old blooms
The more you stop them going to seed.

Children like making rose water
By dunking the heads over night,
Giving the bottles to mother
To use in her cooking – alright!

Summer and autumn they flower,
It's a trait that the roses do well,
Coloured petals form fresh each hour,
When the bush is mature, how they smell!

Sweet Honeysuckle

Honeysuckle, honeysuckle, you're so sweet,
Leaving others in the shade,
Honeysuckle, honeysuckle – lovers meet
In a garden glade.

Such heady scent is scarce to find,
It hits you with a zing,
Full of honey and sugary tones,
No wonder insects sing!

Honeysuckle, honeysuckle, climbs up walls,
Places other plants don't dare,
Opening dainty white/pink flowers,
Perfuming evening air.

Tommy's Pet Toad

Tommy had a pet toad,
He rescued it when it was crossing the road.
He picked it up, put it in a bucket,
Took it to his garden. He learned to love it.
The toad hopped about, ate some flies,
Amongst the undergrowth it had a disguise.
Tommy watched as it lay in the pond,
Croaking low, a mate did respond.
After a while the toad had some babies
That swam in the pond, both men and ladies.
Tommy was thrilled and called to his mum:
"Look at the toad-lets, they are having such fun —
Chasing each other in the water,
Growing bigger each day, I think they oughta
Survive and have young of their own.
Isn't it great? Look how they've grown!"
Tommy now has dozens of toads,
Starting from one that was crossing the road.
They hop in his garden and eat all the slugs,
The garden has flourished as toads also eat bugs.
Now Tommy keeps toads for years to come
And gets lots of praise for it from his mum.

Plastic Plums?

Are they plastic?
No, they're real.
Take a look,
Yes, have a feel.

Decoration
For my chums?
These are not
Your plastic plums.

Suck the goodness
From this fruit.
Eat the flesh –
Don't stain your suit.

See how juicy
They've become:
The real Mc Coy,
Not plastic plums.

Whopping great parsnips

A surprise will come, you'll never guess,
Parsnips now growing, just impress.
They're over two and one half pounds,
These whopping veg dug from the ground.

The top leaves slowly dying back
Due to frosts that have attacked.
Leaving these roots so good and sweet
For Sunday roast, so fine to eat.

The autumn and the winter's cold
But good for root crops, so be bold –
Go out amongst the garden weeds,
See what you've grown from summer seeds.

Get the spade and dig around,
Pull the parsnips from the ground.
You never know what's under there,
Maybe a whopper you all can share.

Natural Autumn

Creepy little crawly things,
Under rocks and stones –
Woodlouse, spiders, ants and more,
Looking for a home.

Rotting leaves, and little twigs,
Decaying slowly there.
Micro-fauna chomping mad
Beneath the autumn air.

A blackbird pecks, and pecks, and pecks,
In the understory,
Looking for some tiny grubs –
Magnificent in glory.

Heartened by still warming sun
Before the cold, cold chills,
Mushrooms and other fungi come,
Red caps above their gills.

Berries from the hawthorn bush
Glow with a tangy smile.
Field mice and a flock of birds
Eye this fruitful isle.

Feeding up, and breaking down,
The cycle never ends.
Days grow shorter, winter waits,
Nature just attends.

Man Up For Fruit

Oranges are not the only fruit –
There's figs and mangos and all,
And apples and pears, and grapes so sweet,
On trees and vines that grow small.

Aromatic and succulent berries
Are judged by many the best,
Packed with vitamins and element traces,
They put healthy hairs on your chest.

So curl up one night with a juicy fruit
Fresh from the tree, in a pie,
Or a banana or kiwi, all squidgy and ripe,
They give you a beautiful high.

Barley

Barley swaying in the breeze –
A country field just lined with trees.
Big harvester's sythe from far and near,
This barley will soon become a beer.

Hoppy tints and malty tones
Go to take away our groans.
At 9 o' clock we do appear
In the local for a beer.

Chatting, drinking, having fun,
The bar maids work is never done.
Light the fire now winter's here -
A cosy, cosy atmosphere.

Have some snacks, or have a meal,
Let your spaniel come to heel.
Passing time with warmth and cheer,
Supping on that tasty beer.

Cool Bare Feet

Cool bare feet on new-mown grass,
Cotton clothes and pale straw hats,
On hot, hot days in city parks,
Slumbering on seaside mats.

White ice cream and strawberry sauce,
Nuts and sprinkles on the top,
Loving each mouthful, of course,
Dripping cream when sun is hot.

Factor fifty on our skin,
Golden bronze, a perfect tan,
Freckled noses and cheeks begin
On pretty children's faces and hands.

Go to the beach or to the pool,
Take a dip, yes have a swim,
Aunties, Mums, one and all,
Swimsuits on, summer begins!

Chocolate

Chocolate is the sweet of dreams,
A true delight: the cocoa bean.
A bar of dark, or creamy milk
In the evening tastes like silk.
Melting gently in your mouth,
A chocolate bar here in the South,
And in the North, and East, and West,
Is like heaven, it leaves the rest.
Eating chocolate before bed
Sends a message to your head.
The unctuousness for sure
Will leave your mouth just wanting more.
So when the daytime gets you down
Turn to chocolate to banish frowns.

Indulge in chocolate once in a while
And feel no guilt, put on a smile,
As chocolate is the sweet of dreams,
A true delight: the cocoa bean.

Hallowe'en

Pumpkins carved and lit with candles
Flickering beneath the door frame handles.
Gouls, and witches casting spells,
Ghostly forms, black cats, and hell
Make up the evening filled with fright,
Hallowe'en – a dark October night.

When the knock comes upon your door
Give face-painted children sweets, and more
Chocolate than they can eat-
Little ones, with Mums - for trick or treat.

Then realise the ghost of Auntie Mabel
Is in your house around the table,
Making cups and saucers shake,
Deforming paintings, nerves soon break.
Dogs start howling, cats miaow,
The supper burns, and house plants bow.

At bedtime this night, try not to dream
Bad things in sleep, on Hallowe'en.

In The Surgery

Waiting in a whitewashed waiting room -
Coughs and colds and rheumatism
The main complaint.
It's the winter chill.
Doctors and nurses calling names.
The patients emerge every ten minutes,
Holding prescriptions.
Sneezing.
Germs abound (such little molecules).

My turn now –
The nurse asks my problem?
Going to a cupboard
She takes out a syringe and a tray.
She slowly injects warm water
Into my ears. It swirls while
Lumps of wax are washed out
Onto the tray.

Smiles all round, because at last
I can hear everything –
Even the distant call of blackbirds outside,
As I walk away.

On ScrobySands

Grey seals call out from a sand bar
To pups fishing for the first time,
While tourists look over just so far
Binoculars poised in a line.

Herring is being devoured,
Tackled by seal pups at sea.
Seagulls come by the hour -
They screech and dive angrily.

Tourists take photos of all this,
Bobbing about on their boats.
The sunshine and light wind is just bliss,
Distant swimmers hold onto their floats.

This scene off East Anglia's coastline
Of our population of seals
Sees nature and tourism combine, to
Watch mammals with young having meals.

Pineapple Airways

Pineapple Airways flies the lucky few
To island destinations. It has a crew
Of jolly folk tending to every need and whim,
To castaways, conservationists, her and him.
So off to the Maldives, Sechelles, Caribbean and Pacific Isles,
Flying quickly gives many joyous smiles.
Sunshine always, sometimes tropical rain,
But heat and sand and blue sea remain.
Flying boats land on the sea,
Pineapple Airways is the one for me!

The Canal Trip

This week is the date of our holiday trip –
A canal boat, and a birthday today –
We plan to have a rare old time, with no lip,
From our wives and our girlfriends – okay?

Setting off slow from the old boatyard
Near Birmingham, heading North West.
Three barges in convoy, it will be quite hard,
To work out the route that is best.

Someone's in charge, I do hope they know
The east from west, south from north.
Lucky the speed on canals is so slow,
We set off and tally on forth.

Stopping for beer and wine and food
At a lovely waterside pub.
Chatting with friends, while they're in the mood,
For gossip and drink and some grub.

Back on the boat and the weather has turned
From sunshine to cloud and some rain.
Playing cards down below, we have all learned
That good weather is forecast again.

On the tiller at the back of these long boats
Is a driver bearing all of the weather.
They steer their barge even when they are soaked,
And get to the end of their tether.

A lock gate approaches, there's no turning back,
The driver puts the boat into reverse.
It stops and then glides between the gap
Of the lock walls, water slowly dispersed.

Chugging along through country and towns,
Breathing fresh air cracks a smile.
Herons and swans know no bounds,
Kingfishers come out for a while.

This week is the date of our holiday time,
Twenty lock gates behind us, you know?
At the end of this time we are sailors so prime,
And are sad to pack up and go.

The Village Show

Rows of good-looking vegetables,
Fruit, jam, bread, cakes and scones,
Handicrafts, flowers on trestle tables,
Waiting to be judged alone.

Village people pit their skills
In this yearly show and fete.
Lovely sunshine fits the bill,
Exhibitors can just stand and wait.

Come in and view, when doors are opened,
Pay a meagre 50p.
The judging enclave now has spoken –
Winners there for all to see.

Have the carrots or the longest bean
Outshone the rest and come in first?
Maybe the cake from Mrs Dean?
Or wine from Charlie? Our children's verse?

The photo taken by my best friend?
The knitting by Auntie May?
The flower arrangement: "Without Ends"?
The pottery dish in porcelain clay?

If you win, or come in second,
Get commended, or take a cup,
You could be a growing legend,
With gardening on the up and up.

But whatever, come what may,
Enjoy yourself if you can.
Possibly it's not your day,
You may be an also-ran.

Have some tea and a big cake,
Don't shed a cold lonely tear.
You may have made a slight mistake,
It could be better next year.

Partners

Beauty in a slow dance,
Movement: touching everywhere.
Beauty in a quick glance,
Or reflected in a mirror's glare.

Beauty of some soft lips,
Giving such a warm kiss.
Beauty of child-bearing hips,
Swaying that way and this.

Beauty in a loving heart,
Kindness there, so warm and true.
Beauty right from the very start,
Loving partners, me and you.

GLORIOUS POEMS (2016)

West Country Brew

Rosy, russet, green they be
Freshly picked from yonder trees.
The farmer and her family
Gathering fruit down in the Lea.

Worcester Pearmain, Bramley, Cox,
Assorted others in a box.
Handling should avoid the knocks:
Here comes the farmer; the girl, the fox.

She brings another apple sack,
Heaves the contents from her back:
"These for cider, they've been attacked
By the wasp – it is a fact!"

Apple juice now is flowing
The farmer has a way of knowing
It's a good year, her face is glowing,
Content, her happiness is showing.

Soon the cider-making's done
And helpers rest beneath warm sun,
Drinking last year's brew, the fun
Of apple picking has now run.

The farmer gives them all a kiss,
Her head spins round in rising mist:
Menfolk, and the little Miss,
Brothers and her darling sis.

Rosy, russet, green they be
Freshly picked from yonder trees,
When dew was dripping lusciously,
Delicious fruit and cider see.

The Batty Biologist

Down the path, bringing shade,
A line of poplar trees parade.
They stand so tall like lolly-pop sticks,
Until in a dip a little house sits.
Its roof is slate, its walls white stone,
An old Professor called it home.

She lived alone with all her cats,
Her papers, books, and lots of bats.
She sang and liked a jolly dance
When writing to her son in France.
Then watched the bats come out at night,
Skimming low in pale twilight.
The line of poplar trees alive,
As busy as a bees' beehive.

The lady thought it very fine
Studying creatures all the time –
Writing books and giving talks
About her epic wildlife walks.

One day she went, long, long ago,
To a cave down deep below
A valley entwined nearly in green,
Filming bats, as yet unseen.
Swooping, diving, around her head,
Screeching like the real un-dead.
Professor Clare loved every second
"I've found a new sort of bat," she reckoned.

This bat was then named after her,
She was so proud, but did prefer
Climbing mountains, sailing seas,
She studied creatures while on her knees.
But never did she find another
Animal waiting to be discovered.

She looked and looked, saw many things,
Including mammals with reptile wings.
When she retired to the countryside,
Her talks drew folk from far and wide.
They listened to her daring tales
In England, Scotland, and in Wales.

She talked about her love and passion
For animals, in everyday fashion.
Now people are very much aware,
Of tree-dwelling bats, and those named 'Clare'.

Children's Children

The thunderstorm panics the dogs
The cows, the sheep and the hogs.
Crashing spikes of white
And rain with all of its might.
The thunderstorm comes overhead.
There is shelter in an old shed, as
Pellets of rain fall on down,
Belting the roof and the ground.
Counting the time in-between
The rumbles and lightning, it seems
To show us five seconds or more
Between them, down here on the floor.

Suddenly, a bolt from the sky
Passes outside, and I try
To search for a bucket. You see
The bolt has set fire to a tree,
Splitting the trunk to the core
Like a sharp axe-head or chainsaw.
But, the torrential rain lashes hard
And douses the fire near the yard.
The storm passes by and we see
What is left of our smouldering tree.

Standing a century there,
Burned down without any care.
Silhouetted as the night falls
Like a ghost that just simply appals.
The Oak might not grow any more
But the sculptural timber is sure
To be crafted into beautiful things –
Wooden bowls, and cups, even rings.
Now sunshine starts very bright,
Sparking life in the saplings that might
Take over from our old tree
For our children's children to see.

The Spider's Prey

October sees the spider try
And catch some insects passing by
In its dewy mesh of silk,
Tight as rope - especially built —
The spider wraps around its prey
A cocoon so fine, it will delay
The insect corpse from going far —
Like locking it in a little jar.

As slow mists rise, sun appears,
The birds sing sweetly, bringing cheer.
The spider sucks its catch here dry
And waits for something else to fly
Into the web when passing through,
Sticking legs, like in a glue.
Struggling makes the body stay,
Another insect has had its day.

The cunning spider ties up its catch,
Repairs the web, and notes the match:
This insect is too large to eat
In one go, but what a treat!
Cocooned in silken threads it lasts
A week or so as a cast.
The spider hides down in its web
As passing insects float and ebb.

This dewy web is stretched and torn,
The spider spins again at dawn.
Repairs the silk between two stems,
This trap is primed once again.
Another morning, mists are still,
The cunning spider up for a kill.
Small flying creatures will beware
The spider and the spider's lair.

Snakes In The Sand

There was a massive boa constrictor
Who had a brother and a sister.
Kept by Trevor and his son
In separate tanks, as they were long.

They had plenty of good food to eat –
Little mammals were a welcome treat.
Squeezing tight and gulping down,
Mice and rabbits from outside of town.

Trevor let them out sometimes
Each snake could slither and it could climb.
But, one day as the sun shone brightly
The constrictors slithered all too sprightly.

Outside the house, to the long grass,
Down the path, they didn't ask.
They moved beyond the garden gate,
Three snakes who really could not wait.

Into the street, and to the park,
Waiting there until the dark.
But the boa constrictors then got cold
As the moon came out, so they dug holes

In the sand of the park sand pit –
Three snakes huddled and did sit.
Meanwhile, Trevor was so distraught:
"Where have they gone?" was his only thought.

He searched his garden and all his house,
Tempting them with a dead white mouse.
Until the sun came out next morning,
The snakes awoke without warning

.

Little Ella was digging in the sand,
With a bucket and spade clutched in her hands.
She dug and dug, and dug up the snakes,
Before realizing her mistakes,

Six steely eyes looked at her, still,
Their forked tongues flashing fast, until
The police and an ambulance were called
As Ella was shaking, she was appalled.

Crying now, the girl did plea:
"Those snakes were much bigger than me!"
A warning went out in the town
Trevor and his son came on down

To the park, and there they did spot
Three Boa's who, like it or not,
Were climbing up upon the slide,
To come on down for a good ride.

Trevor had brought a big brown sack
And bagged the snakes to take them back.
The children all cheered him, before
Trevor took them to his door.

He put them each back in his house
Under warm lights, with a dead mouse.
And the boa constrictors did stay
And feed and drink for much of the day.

Now then, the massive boa constrictor,
With his brother, and his big sister
Stayed quietly looking for some peace,
Not waiting for another release.

As they settled down to sleep,
The snakes had memories to keep.
Remembering how they got so cold
The Boa's didn't have to be told.

They'd stay there in their cosy warm tanks
Be fed quite often, and not play pranks.
Satisfied snakes not wanting more,
The community now secure, for sure.

Dreams

I want to sing, I want to cry
Every time you catch my eye.
I want to kiss, I want to love
Your very essence passing by.

I have missed you all these years,
Five hundred miles apart it seems,
But every day glad thoughts appear
And every night you're in my dreams.

Timothy Blake fell for Catherine Morton

Timothy Blake fell for Catherine Morton
When he was out shopping, as leaves fell, in autumn.
Timothy Blake bought a couple of shirts,
While Catherine tried on a new skirt.
As they emerged from their changing compartments,
They bumped into each other and both were startled.
Timothy Blake knocked Catherine's skirt from her hands,
He picked it up like a chivalrous man.
Catherine Morton felt love at first sight,
She thanked him and gave him a smile so white.
He looked deep in her eyes and wanted to kiss her,
He too was smitten, he knew he would miss her.
So taking her hand, he asked for her number,
She coyly told him, her heart raced like thunder.
Now Timothy Blake loves Catherine Morton,
He doesn't regret going shopping in autumn.
They have a baby called little Rose,
A name that Catherine's mother chose.
They live in a flat quite near to the park,
So the three of them walk there until the dark,
Then go inside, put baby to bed,

Open some wine and toast cheese on white bread.
Timothy Blake loves Catherine Morton,
Yes, Timothy Blake loves Catherine Morton,
Young lovers together, since leaves fell, last autumn.

Scurrilous Deception

Michael likes to bathe in the sun,
Kerry rubs cream on his chest,
Michael lays on a sunbed for fun,
While Kerry says reading is best.

In Majorca, this month it boils,
Kerry and Michael agree,
It is best to be covered in oils,
Or to bask in the shade of a tree.

Michael sips gin and cool tonic
And Kerry likes passion fruit fizz,
These hard toiling Cambridge accountants
Working for folk in show biz.

Kerry and Michael are lovers,
He hopes this news doesn't travel.
If his wife in Cambridge discovers
His partnership here will unravel.

He taps out a quick email
Saying: "I wish you were here."
Deception on a grand scale, he
Kisses Kerry's mouth and her ear.

His wife back in Cambridge taps back:
"Yes, I miss you more than lots!"
Then she quickly puts on her thin mac,
Rushing out to collect the young tots.

Kerry is Michael's work partner
Who is also sharing his bed,

A big bosomed girl with red garters,
Not caring where she lays her head.

Michael and Kerry start caressing:
"This business trip is such fun,
Majorca is never depressing,"
Says Michael before he is done.

Michael and Kerry are lovers
They slowly tan in the rays.
His wife will soon discover
That he is a slob who betrays.

Derek and the Fog

Looking out onto murk and fog,
A man is walking with his dog.
The few street lights in a long line
Giving the pavement an orange shine.
The dog is panting, walking fast,
His little legs going, he's aghast.
The man pulls up his raincoat hood,
The fog encloses him well and good.
He hurries on to a lighted shop,
Its lights a-glowing, a welcome stop.
He buys some mints and a daily paper,
Looks at the headlines – the usual capers.
The terrier waits outside the door,
Resting his backside on the floor.
The dog looks and yaps a bit,
"Good boy," says Derek, "Good boy to sit."
They disappear into the fog:
Derek and his little dog.

Walking slowly in a loop
Derek's thoughts of warming soup
And white cut bread made into toast
Overcome him quickly, like the most
Exotic place that he's ever been,

Or watching TV when the Queen
Gave stirring words and nearly cried
Soon after Princess Diana died.

He leaned down, picked up his dog,
Unlocked his house there in the fog.
"Come on now, we're home again."
He called the terrier by its name.
Charlie yapped, waiting to see
What Derek and him would have for tea:
Some crunchy biscuits for the dog, and some
Oxtail soup - to shut out the fog.

Sunflowers

A gift of sunflowers
To brighten up an Autumn day.
Orange shining sunflowers
Gleaming on my shelf.
I never expected sunflowers –
Or anything.
Your kindness brings sunshine
As the rain falls.
So thank you, thank you, thank you.
Yes, thank you, for the gift of sunflowers.

Titan Arum

On Saturday evening, an almighty pong
Hung in the air – but what was wrong?
Smelly feet or rotten eggs?
Sulphurous tints or drainpipe dregs?
The Titan Arum caused quite a stir,
Thousands of people overheard, that
This was the time the lily flowered
At Cambridge Botanics. The crowd perspired,
But caught a glimpse, and one large whiff
From this rare horticultural gift.
A phallic tower; gargantuan spathe,

Is what this plant grew to save.
Pollination by some trusted flies
Before the flower withered, then died.
So, on Saturday evening, the outrageous pong
Proved the contrary; there's nothing wrong.

The Wonderful Emma

I saw her reading the *Sunday Times,*
An elegant lady just in her prime.
She smiled and muttered several words,
The café was full, but I listened and heard, that
She worked as a writer for the *Daily News,*
Dressed in a smart suit, and her stunning red shoes.
She said to me she was late –
Her deadline was coming – I could just relate
To that, as I am a writer too,
She left her coffee, reached for her shoe.
She picked up her bag from under the table
And combed her hair, and adjusted a label
At the back of her jacket, for it could be seen,
She put on some lipstick, and towards me she leaned.
Speaking so softly: "It'll be published tonight,"
I nodded and thanked her: "Yes, fine, alright."

Packing up her laptop and saying 'goodbye',
The journo left with a tear in her eye.
Our meeting had gone so very smooth,
But my harrowing tale had left her quite moved.

Next day in the paper I read the feature –
A double page spread with a really good picture
Of me and her chatting over a drink,
The piece was so gripping, it did make me think.
She captured my tone, and with her really sharp views
Brought the story to life, this interview
Couldn't have gone better, it'll be a best-seller
Thanks to the *News* writer – the wonderful Emma.

Reminiscences

Alice and Lulu met at secondary school,
Now it is all over, they sit and recall
How they talked French in their Spanish classes,
To annoy Ms Stevens in her horn-rimmed glasses.
Soaking loo paper and moulding some balls
Before caking them on the school toilet walls.
Alice and Lulu liked to play tricks
On Mr Mac Donald and Mrs Jane Pitts:
Their science lessons were spiced up one time
By doing experiments with acid and lime.
And as for the monotonous Geography teacher
Who on Sunday mornings was a church woman preacher,
The girls fell asleep a number of times
Then were abruptly awakened and told to do lines.

Now, sitting in a café with a hot skinny latte,
Alice and Lulu, just out of Pilates,
Reminiscing on school days, when who should appear,
But their old Form Mistress, now an old dear.
Saying 'Hello' and shaking her hand
The women can now really understand
What a handful they were, how they used to be,
Having told Miss Mullen, she also agreed.

Alice and Lulu now have girls of their own
Going through school, and starting to moan.
It seems teenage girls are much worse than boys
"but, my how quick they grow out of their toys!
From little princesses prancing around,
To horrible madams ruling the ground."
"Like mother, like daughter," Miss Mullen replies,
She wants to smile but tears well in her eyes:
"I saw you both as time passed along,
From childhood to grown-up, your innocence gone."

Alice and Lulu looked down at their shoes
Before finishing their coffee and making a move.
Flustered, embarrassed, and in a great whirl
Miss Mullen calls out: *"You're always my girls!"*

Alice and Lulu had now turned a page
They mention Miss Mullen, and how she has aged.
Time had mellowed this once feared young teacher
And she had turned into a sweet, gentle creature.

It just goes to show, back when you were sixteen
The world seems so different, and you can be truly mean.

Books

Books are one of life's simple pleasures,
From Jackie Collins to Measure for Measure.
But our Council is considering cuts
To library services – are they just nuts?

A child growing up loves a picture book;
Chasing pirates like Captain Hook.
How could the Council take this away?...
Deprive poor children, who just may
Be captains of industry one day,
With classic books leading their way:
Black Beauty's adventures, or Mr Tom,
While Kerouac's rebellion still goes on.
Poetry, memoir and science tomes
Free from the library, to bring to our homes.
Economics, art and geography books,
Philosophy and classics not overlooked.
A great world of learning in one place,
More cuts to our libraries would be a disgrace.

They say they need to consider new things
To make some money, then see what this brings,
Like a business centre, where corporate need
Runs hand-in-hand with the books that we read.
This privatisation forced on us this way
Omits the fact that the taxes we pay
Should be enough for community space
And libraries for all, in every place.
As books are one of life's great pleasures,
Whether it's Ms Collins, or even Measure for Measure.

Have You Seen David Attenborough?

Have you seen David Attenborough?
He's counting flamingo's, and being so thorough.
From African plains, to a water hole,
To countryside with ratty and mole.
Rhinoceros, ape, and hopping kangaroo,
Elk and platypus, via Wooloomooloo.
Tiger and lion and a playful lemur,
Camouflaged insects, to creatures with fur.
Fishes and coral and octopi
Can each be said to have caught his eye.
Travelling far, but always with cheer,
David Attenborough is so, so welcome here.
He is a naturalist/broadcaster who wants us to see
The life on our planet, from animal to tree.
Birds like the duck, and the golden eagle
Are subjects as much as a soppy pet beagle.
Recordings of nature for sound and TV,
Professionally produced by our own BBC.
David Attenborough and team are more than OK,
So the world salutes them, "Hooray, yes, Hooray!"

Green and Gold

Australian tourists, green and gold
Witnessed collapse of batting bold
At Trent Bridge, Nottingham: August 6.
While Stuart Broad here bowled for kicks –
15 scored, 8 wickets had,
Oz out for 60 runs; that's bad!

Australian cricketers had no luck,
So many good players with just a duck, while
England fans watched with much glee,
Something they only dreamed to see.
And even Geoffrey Boycott smiled, and said:
"They need to bat here with their head.
Technique is key on English grounds,
Nicking a swinger will bring on frowns."
Geoffrey, Geoffrey, you're always right,
These Englishmen gave Oz a fright.
Test cricket of the highest grade
From Cook and Co, history made.
The Ashes series will now be won,
2015, in August sun.

The Letter

I really don't know why you won't talk to me?
Is it because you found the cat had a flea?
But this is no reason to go silent, you see.
Oh, I really don't know why you won't talk to me?

I really don't know why you have the grumps?
Is it because my custard had lumps?
But this is no reason to get down in the dumps.
Oh, I really don't know why you have the grumps?

I really don't know why you cropped your long hair?
Is it because you want to see if I care?
But this is no reason to play 'truth or dare'.
Oh, I really don't know why you cropped your long hair?

I really don't know if you want me at all?
Is it so strange we still tumble and fall?
I think this is the reason our love will stand tall.
These moments are life, now dearest, please call.

The Summer Ball

She sparkles like the champagne she sips,
Elegant in a swan-white summer gown.
She beams.
The marquee draped with coloured ruffs,
And shocking-red roses, as
Dance music penetrates my pulsing heart.
Buffet niblets for all. Smart waiters and
Waitresses mingle
Through the people traffic.
Flute glasses lined up in endless rows on
Starched-cloth tables,
Ready to be filled with bubbly.
Dior ladies perfume wafts around in the breeze.

She smiles as we dance:
Wonderland!

Heady now, friends congregate in the night air
To watch fireworks crackle and bang
In the sky, like ephemeral stars.
Still elegant, but flagging, she removes her heels
And falls into an embrace.

Slowly we head home across the cobbles of old streets.
A night to cherish, a night at the summer ball.

Friend

Meeting after all this time
Is such a wonderful surprise;
Meeting after many years
Chased tears into my eyes.
Although you have cut your hair
And lost a pound or two,
I recognised you instantly
After calling from the blue.
Your youthful looks still intact,
Your sense of fun is true.
We laughed, not putting on an act
And shared a drink or two.

Remember when we were so young,
Big student loyalty –
Unseparable, we made our home
Together, you and me.
Until the final moment came
Our courses at an end,
Then losing touch, a hideous shame,
Letters I could not send.
I realised this sudden loss,
Our friendship had been betrayed
By each of us, now in the world,
Hefty decisions made.

Now with employment and work to do,
Partners don't seem to stay.
A move to Bath, then on to Crewe,
Failed marriage on the way.
Life to be lived by one and all,
Settled now, I smile
When answering your unexpected call
And chatting to you a while.
Time seems to just slip on by,
You proved to be my friend,
Indeed, we didn't have to try
When meeting last weekend.

Christine And The Birds

Walking in the crisp springtime air
Christine moves quickly, then stops and stares.
A robin and a bold blackbird
Are near, and can just be heard
Flapping their wings while on the ground
In a bath that they have found.
Cleaning their feathers, Christine thinks,
She rubs her eyes and then she blinks.
The birds take wing and off they fly,
Christine smiles; waves them goodbye.

Now to the office where she will
Be at the beck-and-call of Bill.
Then home-time comes, and off she trots,
She sees some thrushes with their spots
On their throats, hopping along
In the car park, looking strong.

Christine sighs, she's thrilled to bits,
Realising these birds will soon have chicks.
She gets into her motor car
Feeling privileged, like a star,
As birdsong twitters everywhere
Christine just listens, she stops, she stares.

An Actor's Life

At three 'o clock this afternoon
A shaft of light pierced my room.
Curtains flung back as I arise;
An actor's life I do surmise!

Working halls and live theatre,
Singing songs in every meter.
Playing Hamlet, and then a clown,
Each week it changes in this town.

Tonight my accent is deep Fen,
My entrance scene is played again.
People come to see me ramble,
I am a cop; Inspector Randall.

Bungling cases, then success:
Miss Marple would be so impressed!
I love the clapping from the crowd,
We take our bow, feeling proud.

Then travelling home in my old car
To see my kitten, Balthazar.
The night is cold, it's nearly three,
My kitten is here, on my knee.

I sip some vino 'Espanol',
The kitten thinks I am his doll.
Razor needles pierce my skin,
But I am calm deep within.

Night owls hoot, it is bedtime,
I finish off my blood-red wine.
Take Balthazar his little toy,
To watch him play is such a joy.

I say goodnight and shut the door
Thinking of tonight's applause:
An aged actor's life to stay –
Tomorrow it's a matinee.

Inquisitive Alice

Alice, Alice, Alice, inquisitive little girl
Sees a 'Drink Me!' potion, and a different world unfurls.
Out of some woods, a Cheshire cat beams its certain smile,
Come, come my dear, it seems to say, be with us a while.
Into a place all set for tea, with eccentric characters:
A dormouse and a mad hatter, a timepiece softly whirrs.
"I'm late!" is heard, "I'm late!" again, "No time to stop and stare."
Alice calms them down for sure, her grace beyond compare.
As dormouse slowly stirs once more from a gentle slumber,
March hare runs round: "There's tea and cake for all, sandwiches with
cucumber."
"I'm late! I'm late!" echoes again, "There really is no time
For eating cake and drinking tea, in reason or in rhyme."
Then from the woods the Cheshire cat beams its certain smile,
A wicked Queen, flamingo golf, card regiments in aisles.
The Jack of Hearts bowing low, the Queen is most displeased,
Alice jumps once, then again, "Off with her head!" decreed.
"You cannot chop off my head," Alice sternly cries,
The Queen repeats "Off with her head!", the Jack of Hearts just sighs.
Alice is mesmerised by this, but she stands her ground,
Her head really must stay put, the befuddled Queen just frowns.
This place is just beyond the pale, a magic wonderland:
Mad Hatter, Cheshire Cat, card Queen, March Hare and Dormouse
stand.
Alice, Alice, Alice, inquisitive little girl,
Enticed by the 'Eat Me!' snack, her mind still in a whirl.
What treats to come beyond this world? Imagination wild,
Adventures for every one of us, release our inner child.

November Baking

It really is a time for baking,
And Christmas cake is what we're making.
Ingredients like flour and eggs,
Spices, currants, and brandy dregs
Make a mixture that's for tasting,
Smooth, delicious; none for wasting.

Let it rest for a short while,
Then once in the oven crack a smile, as
Aroma fills the kitchen spaces,
Cake is cooking, indulgence graces.
Family congregate once more,
So leave ajar the kitchen door.
The smell permeates all round,
Upstairs, in bedrooms, and in the lounge.

After some hours cooking is stopped,
Now perfection – a golden top!
Cooled, and put inside a tin
Then fed with brandy deep within,
Weekly, up until it's right
For icing, which is just alright:
Father Christmas deep in white snow,
With a message: "Ho, Ho, Ho, Ho."
Happy Christmas it has to be,
A worthy cake for festive tea.

Enjoyed by family and friends,
Baking perfection just depends
On a good recipe, and care,
You'll have a cake you all can share.

Memories

The weekend has gone so very fast
But memories I have are sure to last.
A hug and kisses from a friend,
Two joyful days that can't extend.
You caught the train on Sunday eve,
Apart again, but I believe,
Together, the magic; yes, the spark,
Between us, and our happy lark
Exists, and is so worthwhile,
Thinking of you just brings a smile.
I know we are not partners now
But for your company I take a bow.
Friendship is a good thing for sure,
This weekend left me wanting more
Because memories are here to last
As time just passes by so fast.

She Is The One

She is the one; the only one:
Talking, laughing, full of fun.
She makes me bright at times of stress,
Warm hugs soothe my inner mess.
She's crazy sometimes, this I know,
But beautiful with her friendly glow.
In winter, summer, autumn and spring
She is there, a constant zing.
On her computer keyboard tapping
Her words of wisdom, nothing lacking.
She is comforting to me –
A woman whom I seldom see.
But her company makes my heartbeat rev,
She is the one; the only Bev.

Fancy Dress

He met her at a fancy dress
Occasion at college. He more or less
Fell in love with her right there –
Her longing eyes and shining hair.

She wore a wet-suit with a zip
Up the front, very hip
He thought, and his advances
Were met with laughs and sideways glances.

He got her a drink, and then they talked,
His beer, her half, outside they walked
Down to her cottage under clear skies,
The moon so brilliant, he surmised

She liked him, maybe for just a while,
He kissed her cheek and made her smile.
He said goodbye there at her gate,
The air was chilled, it was quite late.

They both agreed they'd had a ball,
They'd meet tomorrow by the hall
Before their lectures, dead on nine,
A parting look, she was sublime.

And in the morning they both appeared,
They fell in love for several years.
A perfect couple, so it seemed,
Full of fun and future dreams.

Until the end came and he did cry,
After her Finals she said goodbye.
They parted, went their separate ways,
But still in love, he still displayed

His peacock feathers in piles of letters,
But no reply, she had found a better
Man than him, he was so upset,
What to do, he had to let
Her live her life as she chose,
Set her free, his perfect rose.
This flower for him forever will bloom
Until black shadows near his tomb

Remind him of her; she is his friend
In his head, until life ends.
A vision that for him impressed
Her wet-suit choice for fancy dress.

Burst Pipes

Crispy air grabbed her nose,
Her fingers went numb as house pipes froze.
Sweating, coughing while in bed,
Her dog brings comfort, but her head
Is throbbing, and it's so, so hot,
Mopping her brow, looking a lot
Like an explorer in the cold
Wearing a scarf tucked in the folds
Of blankets all around her frame.
Winter cold that then became
A nightmare as her house did flood
When pipes thawed out, her very blood
Boiled today in winters chill
She often said she was never ill.
But now this nightmare is quite real,
The plumbing has failed, it's quite surreal
To lay in bed all a-shiver
With cold water like a river.

Getting higher, so her toes
Felt colder than her running nose.
Out of bed into this hell,
Slopping around, it's hard to tell
If her slippers are still here,
Sodden, her carpet now appears

Like a reef below the waves
Of cold, cold water that behaves
Like an ocean or a sea
In her house, up to her knee.

Picking up the mobile phone
She called a plumber, had a moan.
Coughing more, she bowed her head,
A moment of reverie here instead.
Mourning all that she had lost,
A winter flood brought such a cost.

But help was here in overalls,
A bag of wrenches for his calls.
Soon the pipes were fixed once more
And water mopped out of the door.
The woman coughs and then she sneezes
Opening doors so winter breezes
Fill the house and hope to dry
The carpets, but the winsome sky
Does not bring warmth, but may bring snow,
She has to leave, yes, she must go.

Cold-riddled, but her good friend
Can be relied on till the end.
It won't be long before things dry
And the cold will say goodbye.

Back to normal, it's a good bet
 That this is a winter she won't forget.

Worthwhile

When I think of you
Warm water gushes over me.

When I think of you
There is regeneration of a fading flower.

When I think of you
My pulse-rate quickens.

When I think of you
Joy cascades through my heart.

When I think of you
Endless adventures come to life.

When I think of you
My life is again worthwhile.

Trad Music

You're into ukulele picking
Down the pub, with fingers clicking.
Strewn hops decorate the bar-room walls
And pictures from nature, like waterfalls
Adorn this once quite smoky place.
Now folk musicians interlaced
With singers enjoying some real ale beer
Come together for some hearty cheer.

Ukelele's, fiddles, and guitars, with
Swinging widows from the stars,
Enjoying the Sunday lunchtime session,
Right into evening, at eleven.

Then stagger home down cobbled streets:
A joyful group who often meet
At the bakers, or at the store,
To banter, and to sing some more.

With your ukelele picking,
Joining villagers with fingers clicking,
To keep the old, old ways alive,
Trad music has once more arrived.

Midnight Roses

Midnight roses
Kisses
You're the one.

Gifted posies
Kisses
Still my sun.

Cold days
Warm nights
Loving all the time.

Midnight roses,
Kisses
Still you shine.

Upsetting Gaia

Gaia, our living planet rises
Near a thermal factory ball:
The sunshine warms, but soon surprises –
Now earth's population has to call.

Carbon rising, in its ascendance,
So human beings have a choice,
Captain Cook's oceanic descendants
On atols, now have a loud voice.

Coral dies as seas are warmer,
Polar region's see this too.
Wicked weather belies our karma,
Across the world, patterns anew.

Please think about your daily living –
Petrol fumes, and burning lights
Releasing carbon, so unforgiving
Now Gaia and our sun shine bright.

Heartbreak

Saying you would always be mine,
And loving me all the blessed time.
Then breaking my delicate heart and soul,
By straying away from our fold.
Ripping my life to little shreds,
Wishing that I was almost dead.
It is not very, very kind,
To leave family life behind.
But do you really, really care?
Or are you just so unaware?
Whisky, gin and some beer
Are not what they quite appear.
Constant drinking to an excess
Leaves your life in one big mess.
Now you're throwing it all away,
A drunkard you will have to stay.
Sleeping rough just God knows where?
But do you really, really care?
A bottle has become your shrine,
Your mortality is in decline.
But do you really, really care?
Or are you just plainly unaware?

My Style

Hold on a short while,
I'm just not into style:
Old sweatshirt and some jeans
If you know what this means?
I'm not into style.

You look so very smart
In your skinnies, you're just art,
And those boots are all the rage,
Straight from a magazine page.
You are into style.

I love you in a dress,
A scarf thrown across your chest,
Looking rather cool:
A lady by the pool.
You are into style.

But what do you see in me?
Something others just don't see?
We're a couple holding hands,
A beauty with her man.
I'm happy with my style.

Forever Friends

What can I say to you, my dear?
As anxious moments fill your head,
Remembering family times, so near,
Toddlers jumping on the bed.

Friends, relations come and go,
School and college up and runs,
I'll stay by you, this I know,
When life is shooting all its guns.

Stay positive, my dear, if you will,
You have your busy life to live.
Mournful thinking will not kill
The hope and light I try to give.

Illnesses come to us all,
So share your memories to the end.
Everybody walks, and falls,
Remember today you still have friends.

Gardening With Dad

Gardening is a surreal pleasure
With my dad – he's a real treasure.
At 84 he still sows
Vegetable seeds, and then he shows
Me how to prune a rose just so:
"The buds are precious, let them grow."

I dig our patch, and with a rake
Make a seedbed that will take
Potatoes and some little seeds,
Carefully done, so they will feed
Us in the coming summer months,
The seedbed must be devoid of bumps.

Vegetables and flowers really flourish
In our garden, as we will nourish
And nurture them as they do grow;
Two gardeners, not doing it for show.

My 84-year-old dad
Is active and not a bit sad.
Showing how to get some pleasure
From gardening. It's a thing to treasure.

THE END